In the Future of U.S Economy

Richard .E Nelson

Table of Contents

Is there an increase in US inflation?

The Federal Reserve of the United States faces a challenging job as it prepares to meet on June 14 and 15. The biggest rise in consumer prices since 1981 occurred in May, when they increased 8.6% from a year earlier. In nominal terms, gasoline costs are at an all-time high. Additionally, global unrest is hindering economic expansion. The fact that May's official number is nothing compared to the Great Inflation that American consumers suffered through in the 1970s and early 1980s is consoling. But according to recent study, drawing comparisons between the inflation rates in America over time may be misleading.

Due to statistical modifications made to the consumer-price index (cpi) in the 1980s, such comparisons are risky. For many years, the housing component of the CPI was calculated using costs paid by homeowners, such as home prices, mortgage interest rates, property taxes, and upkeep expenses. But eventually, government statisticians realized that this method overestimated the actual cost of housing. It resulted in an unstable gauge of housing inflation that changed in response to interest rates (increasing sharply during tightening cycles and falling in easing ones). A new method for calculating the consumer price index (cpi) was adopted by the Bureau of Labour Statistics (bls) in 1983. This method used estimates of what homeowners would make if they leased out their properties, or owners' equivalent rent.

The authors of the paper, Marijn Bolhuis, Judd Cramer, and former treasury secretary Larry Summers, rebuilt the cpi for the years 1946 to 1983 using the bls's current technique for estimating housing costs to better understand how this shift may have distorted historical inflation. They discovered that, contrary to what the official statistics would indicate, the double-digit inflation of the 1970s was both lower and less volatile: the peak rate of 14.8% observed in March 1980 would actually have been 11.4%. In June of that year, the highest core inflation rate of 13.6% would have been 9.1%.

As a result, current inflation rates are higher than the official statistics would indicate. What can be learned from this? According to some experts, the Federal Reserve will be able to pull off a "soft landing," which is when tightening monetary policy reduces inflation without hurting growth. This feat has only been accomplished three times since 1945. The present Fed tightening cycle, according to Mr. Summers and his co-authors, will be much more painful. The only way Paul Volcker, the Fed chairman during the Great Inflation, was able to subdue the beast was by plunging the country into a severe slump. The past data may be misleading because it suggests that the Fed had a much more serious inflation issue back then than it does now. The authors caution that in order to reach the 2% inflation target, there must be almost as much disinflation as under Volcker. What aspects of the economy contribute to inflation?

Prices will rise if there is a greater desire to purchase something, or if there is a rise in demand. Another factor that can raise prices is a reduction in supply, such as if it becomes harder to make goods. When there are delays in the transportation or delivery chains, this occurs.

Both of those developments have happened in the past few years. Demand changed at the onset of the pandemic, and we began spending more money on goods rather than services. We were purchasing more automobiles, electronics, and household products. And the price effect was evident. We experienced supply chain disruptions at the same moment. Because there was a greater demand for products, their prices increased as a result of the decreased availability of the materials required for their production.

How has inflation been exacerbated by the conflict in Ukraine?

The war in Ukraine began as we were still coping with the pandemic. This had an effect on food and energy costs. The sanctions imposed on Russia, which supplies oil to the world market, led to an increase in energy costs. Since the price of oil is determined on a global market, any disruption in the availability of oil affects the price of oil globally. A significant portion of the world's wheat exports come from Russia and Ukraine, whose capacity to produce, gather, and export their grain has also been hampered by the conflict.

The Russian invasion of Ukraine has continued to cause global supply chain disruptions. As a result, the prices of essential commodities such as fuel and food have increased globally. For instance, both Russia and Ukraine account for almost one-third of global wheat exports.

How can studying earlier inflationary times aid our understanding of the current situation?

Energy supply was reduced as a result of the OPEC oil crisis, which raised the price of oil and fuel. Additionally, that was another supply limitation. As a result, because fuel was a necessary component of so many goods we produced at the time, many items saw price increases, and inflation skyrocketed.

Therefore, I believe that historical era to be especially pertinent because it sets up how our expectations of inflation are shifting. Every month, researchers from the University of Michigan question a large group of consumers what they predict the inflation rate will be for the following month and the following year. We refer to these solutions as our "inflationary hopes."

The 15 to 20 years of steady inflation that preceded the inflation of the 1970s saw little variation in respondents' responses from month to month. Following 30 years of stable inflation, during which time responses to that query have also remained largely consistent from month to month, we are currently experiencing this episode. Rising prices, initially influenced by supply issues as well as people's inflationary expectations, are thus the similarities. People now anticipate a greater level of inflation than they did a few months ago.

Who is in charge of curbing inflation and what resources do they have?

The Federal Reserve is the main organization responsible for combating inflation in the US. The Federal Reserve's main weapon is the ability to alter interest rates. The Federal Reserve and its use of interest rates are the real changes that count, although some regulatory agencies may be able to modify their rules and slightly lower prices. Either by raising interest rates or by lowering them, the Federal Reserve will either stall the economy or stimulate it.

After that same time in the 1970s, what caused prices to stabilize?

By implementing extremely strict, conservative, and contractionary monetary policies, the Federal Reserve was able to stop that inflation. They raised loan rates to a maximum of 18%. Thus, the interest rates for obtaining a mortgage to purchase a home ranged from 16% to 18%. That abruptly stopped demand, caused the economy to shrink, and started the worst slump since the 1930s. And as a result, there was less of a desire for the goods, which ultimately caused prices to drop.

What's happening to people's expectations is the other component of the puzzle when it comes to inflation. Early in the 1980s, President Ronald Reagan appeared on television from the White House to reassure the public that he was in charge and that the Federal Reserve would find a solution to the issue. Reagan's assurances resulted in a decrease in people's expectations, which some economists think was essential in lowering inflation in the early 1980s along with the changes in interest rates that drove up unemployment.

Can prices be stabilized without triggering a recession?

When less goods and services are created overall each month than the month prior, a recession has occurred. Therefore, month by month, the quantity of products and services that we produce decreases.

What the Fed means by a "soft landing" is that they want to slow the pace of increase.

Therefore, perhaps we could raise the production rate by 1% per year rather than, say, 2% per year from month to month. If that were to happen, there wouldn't be a recession; instead, development would slow down.

The BRICS's plan for the US dollar

One of the biggest dangers to the dollar is the BRICS countries' dedollarization. Building all the necessary facilities will help de-dollarize the global economy. The journal of the Chinese Communist Party urges opposition to the Dollar's hegemony. The BRICS have already established a number of banks and are busy developing a currency.

The Chinese RMB Yuan, the Russian Ruble, the Indian Rupee, the Brazilian Real, and the South African Rand will serve as the basis for the new currency, which will be built on a basket of the currencies of the five-nation group.

Despite the fact that BRICS (Brazil, Russia, India, China, and South Africa) developed numerous de-dollarization initiatives to lower currency risk and evade US sanctions, existing research has not methodically examined BRICS as a rising power de-dollarization alliance. This study creates a framework called "Pathways to De-dollarization" to address this gap and uses it to examine the institutional and market mechanisms developed by BRICS countries at the BRICS, sub-BRICS, and BRICS Plus levels. The BRICS de-dollarization coalition's leaders and adherents are identified, the coalition's strength is evaluated, and it is determined how BRICS mobilizes other stakeholders. To evaluate BRICS activities from 2009 to 2021, the authors use process tracing, content analysis, semi-structured interviews, archival research, and statistical analysis of quantitative market data. They discover that the coalitional de-dollarization efforts of the BRICS have created vital foundations for a potential alternative non-dollar global financial system.

Since the global financial crisis of 2007–2008, the US dollar's dominance and global leadership have come under increased scrutiny. Because this crisis had its roots in the US, questions were asked about the US government's dependability and the wisdom of maintaining the dollar's hegemonic status in the world financial system. Rising powers now have a chance to demand more standing and representation in global governance as a result of this crisis. The first BRIC (Brazil, Russia, India, China) Summit was held in Yekaterinburg in 2009 at the invitation of Russian President Dmitry Medvedev to discuss how to "overcome the crisis and create a fairer international system... and discuss the parameters for a new financial system." The five members of BRIC have accomplished policy coordination in more than 70 issue areas since South Africa joined in 2010, renaming BRIC into BRICS (Reference Kirton and Larionova). Brazilian MFA, 2020; Kirton and Larionova, 2018). The creation of the New Development Bank (NDB), the Contingent Reserve Arrangement (CRA), and numerous other financial coordination mechanisms serve as examples of the financial cooperation as a key accomplishment of BRICS.

Despite the depth of the BRICS nations' financial cooperation and their expanding interconnectedness, research on the BRICS's financial activities is lacking. However, the risks associated with the BRICS' de-dollarization efforts are especially high. Since the US dollar dominates the world's financial and monetary structure, it has an impact on many facets of world affairs. Because of this, the dollar's influence and standing have been crucial to American leadership around the world (see also Reference Helleiner and Kirshner). 2009, p. 1; Helleiner and Kirshner. The NDB's decision to fund in local currencies rather than only using US dollars is just the tip of the iceberg in terms of BRICS' de-dollarization efforts. Footnote1 It is also unclear whether the rapid de-dollarization of Russia and China, which was sparked by those countries' rising hostilities with the United States, is merely a passing trend or signals a larger paradigm shift in world finance. To put this in perspective, the US dollar's proportion of the bilateral trade transaction between China and Russia decreased from nearly 90% in 2015 to 46% in 2020. (Reference SimesSimes, 2020). In addition, China and Russia have introduced their own cross-border payment systems as competition for the Society for Worldwide Interbank Financial Telecommunication (SWIFT) network, which is controlled by the US. In addition, BRICS has developed a shared BRICS Pay system for retail payments and transactions among its members, which has been made possible by the quick development of the financial technology (fintech) industry. These de-dollarization efforts are largely going unnoticed by modern research. Leading these efforts are reform-minded emerging powers, including strategic US rivals, who have voiced dissatisfaction with the current US-led, dollar-based international financial system. Canary in the coal mine? Do these factual examples point to a broader de-dollarization movement?

Can the BRICS de-dollarize the US-led global financial system? is a crucial question that this study aims to address by methodically examining the nature and effects of these activities. The fundamental premise of this research is that the US dollar's status as the world's dominant currency might not last indefinitely. This idea is supported by the US dollar's displacement of the previous hegemonic currency, namely the British pound sterling. The BRICS' combined economic clout makes analyzing their threat to the US dollar's hegemony crucial. BRICS accounts for 24 percent of global GDP and over 16 percent of world trade (BRICS India, 2021). (BRICS India, 2021). Therefore, the de-dollarization efforts of BRICS would have an influence on both intra-BRICS financial relations and global economic relations. Examining BRICS' de-dollarization initiatives can shed light on the more general issue of whether rising powers can win over supporters and drive global change. Can BRICS members who aren't as engaged in the de-dollarization agenda rally them? Can they extend their de-dollarization efforts outside of the BRICS and establish economies of scale across a number of platforms that cut off the United States and other key Western powers, like the Shanghai Cooperation Organization (SCO)?

Research on rising powers and their effects on US global leadership will benefit from new and necessary insights provided by analyzing BRICS as a de-dollarization coalition and how it might mobilize other players. The fundamental tenet of the US dollar's global leadership, its dominance in the world financial system, is examined in this research. For the United States, this issue has significant consequences for national security. In order to legitimately use coercive economic statecraft and punish its enemies, the United States depends on the dollar's position as the world's most important currency. The capacity of the United States to influence the actions of its enemies would be weakened, which might amplify threats to US national security.

We create an analytical framework dubbed "Pathways to De-dollarization" to examine whether BRICS can de-dollarize the US-dominated global financial system. This framework describes how a coalition of rising powers can work toward dedollarization in order to oppose dollar hegemony. This research adds to the body of knowledge already available on the dominant monetary paradigm, currency statecraft, collective financial statecraft, and the political economics of emerging power coalitions. To reduce their rising risk exposure to the dollar's hegemonic power, rising powers can concurrently pursue two sets of risk mitigation strategies that our framework conceptualizes as "go-it-alone" and "reform the status quo." Both make it possible for an alliance of rising powers, like BRICS, to pursue de-dollarization in order to lower their risk exposure to the US dollar and US sanctions. The coalition of rising powers may be able to expand its global influence or, more generally, accomplish greater financial and geopolitical autonomy with the aid of these de-dollarization strategies. Strategies to create and manage brand-new institutions and/or market mechanisms that are not dependent on the dollar are referred to as "go-it-alone" de-dollarization strategies. When confronted with US sanctions, such measures allow coalition members to diversify their currency risks and retain unrestricted access to the global financial system. The development of these initiatives could result in the establishment of a different or parallel system that is not reliant on the US currency or agreements reached by major Western powers. In contrast, coalitional attempts to renegotiate the rules of the current system are referred to as "reform-the-status-quo" initiatives. Such efforts entail collective bargaining with existing powers to lessen the dominance of the US dollar. These reform-focused initiatives would diversify the representation of currencies in the current system if they were to be effective. Our framework then examines institutional and market processes that a rising power coalition might use to try to de-dollarize the current international financial system in light of these two strategies.

The "Pathways to De-dollarization" paradigm is used to analyze the de-dollarization efforts of the BRICS countries. This research thus offers the first comprehensive analysis of de-dollarization initiatives by a coalition of rising powers. We find that BRICS members have shown clear agreement and a strong dedication to promoting the use of local currencies in international settlements and developing a global financial infrastructure that is not based on the dollar. They have pursued both "go it alone" and "reform the status quo" projects at the same time. For instance, the NDB was created by the BRICS to dedollarize development financing. In an effort to dedollarize the world's financial infrastructure, the organization has also been preparing to introduce a common payment framework that can be used in conjunction with a BRICS digital currency. At the sub-BRICS level, dedollarization initiatives have been most prevalent. To dedollarize the world's oil trade, China, for instance, has successfully introduced the yuan oil futures contract. China and Russia have both created their own international texting platforms. BRICS has also collectively sought reformist approaches, such as creating the dollar-based CRA, advocating for the reform of the IMF Special Drawing Rights, and building a BRICS stock exchanges alliance within the existing system. Together, these initiatives indicate that BRICS has not only attempted to reform the existing system to better incorporate its interests but has also created a nascent de-dollarization infrastructure that supports global de-dollarization in the long run. BRICS' collective efforts to create an alternative nondollar financial system have the potential to completely immunize participants from both exchange and sanction risks resulting from the dollar's dominance and US hegemonic position. Long-term, the de-dollarization infrastructure of the BRICS may even serve as the foundation for a larger de-dollarization coalition that encompasses regional organizations. US allies who want more financial independence and to carry on business with nations that are subject to US penalties may find this coalitional de-dollarization infrastructure to be appealing. For instance, Mark Carney, governor of the Bank of England, stated to central bankers at the Jackson Hole Symposium in 2019 that the dominance of the dollar is the "destabilizing asymmetry" that is increasing "at the heart of the international monetary and financial system." He suggested creating a new synthetic hegemonic currency that might be distributed via a network of central bank digital currencies (Reference CarneyCarney, 2019). Similar to this, the BRICS nations are creating a digital money called BRICS Coin that paves the way for digital de-dollarization.

The BRICS members are still unable to completely depart from the current US dollar-based banking system thanks to the nascent de-dollarization infrastructure of the BRICS. Initiatives by the BRICS to dedollarize the current global financial system are primarily taking place at the sub-BRICS level and have not yet attained the necessary economies of scale. The BRICS are unable to come together as a single de-dollarization alliance due to two main obstacles. The first is that some BRICS countries have stronger ties to the United States than to other BRICS members. This is particularly clear in the case of India and its interactions with China and the US. Despite the fact that this prevents BRICS members from implementing a formal, comprehensive de-dollarization plan in the near future, they may still engage in informal de-dollarization efforts. Second, some BRICS countries, like Brazil and South Africa, have economies that are more integrated into the dollar system than others and are less susceptible to US sanctions. As a result, neither a group-level agreement on de-dollarization nor a common sense of urgency to emphasize it exist among the BRICS members. They all want to reduce their reliance on the US currency, but not everyone wants to leave the US-run international financial system. The majority of BRICS members still have significant holdings of US dollar assets in their reserves, so they suffer losses when the US currency declines.

Current cash circumstances cannot be changed anytime soon. Furthermore, the advantages of de-dollarization may not be free. Breaking away from the current global system and market structure built on the dollar is comparable to imposing your own isolation from the current system. The most obvious costs that BRICS would incur from their separation include higher cross-border transaction costs, more expensive capital raising on dollar-based global markets, and decreased competitiveness of their companies in foreign markets due to a lack of dollar funding. It is debatable whether the BRICS governments could honestly enact de-dollarization initiatives at the corporate level, particularly for companies doing business in countries where the US dollar is the dominant and preferred currency. Additionally, during significant economic crises, the dollar is the "safe haven" currency of preference for international investors. Investors flocked to US dollars in anticipation that the dollar would maintain its value during the 2007–2008 global financial crisis and the economic unrest associated with COVID–19 in 2020. The US Federal Reserve increased currency exchange lines with a number of other central banks during both crises to provide dollar liquidity. A non-dollar system would aggravate problems brought on by emergency access to dollar liquidity. Countries are discouraged from voluntarily rebelling against the dollar hegemony by such dedollarization expenses. Even Russia, which is aggressively accelerating its dedollarization process, is not actively pursuing this agenda. "Russia did not want to give up the dollar as the reserve currency or as a method of payment, but it was forced to," Russian President Vladimir Putin said (TASS Russian News Agency, 2021b).

The structure of this Element is as follows: Section 2 makes the claim that there is no comprehensive account for the coalitional behavior of the BRICS in the de-dollarization space in the literature on currency power, economic statecraft, and the BRICS as a group. To close this gap, it offers a fresh analytical framework. In Section 3, the development of de-dollarization in BRICS cooperation is traced, and the group's dedication to de-dollarization is assessed. The BRICS' "stand-alone" efforts to dedollarize by creating new organizations and markets are examined in Section 4. The "reform-the-status-quo" initiatives by the BRICS to undermine the US-led international banking system from within are examined in Section 5. The results are presented in Section 6, which also discusses the implications of the BRICS de-dollarization coalition for US global leadership and offers ideas for future study topics.

BRICS de-dollarizing represents one of the greatest threats to the Dollar. All the infrastructure is being built to de-dollarize the world economy. The Chinese Communist Party's newspaper calls for pushback against the Dollar's hegemony. BRICS are actively building a currency and have already opened multiple banks.

A Challenge for the Coalition in Dedollarization?

The three categories of scholarly work that are most pertinent to analyzing how rising powers might present a coalitional de-dollarization threat are covered in this section: The literature on rising powers and rising power coalitions in international relations, the literature on the BRICS countries, and the literature on currency power, economic statecraft, and the international monetary system. While these three areas of study shed light on some aspects of our research question, none of them specifically handle the issue of monetary coalitions among rising powers, particularly BRICS as a coalition for de-dollarization. We first show the empirical puzzle, then the "Pathways to De-dollarization" framework, and lastly discuss our findings to close this gap.

De: dollarization thriugh BRICS

The emergence of the US dollar as the dominant currency in the world (both as the most widely held reserve currency and as the most widely used currency for international settlement) and its implications for US global leadership have been major areas of focus for current scholarship on international monetary relations, currency power, and economic statecraft. The currency power of the US dollar has been extensively studied by academics in light of the dollar's position as an international currency. Footnote2 Numerous academics have reevaluated the US dollar's position in the world economy and in relation to US leadership since the global financial crisis. They discussed how the US dollar's international use contributed to American hegemony, how the dollar's supremacy gives the US prestige, and how the US has used the dollar to exert its global sway (Reference KirshnerKirshner, 2008; Reference GoldbergGoldberg, 2011; Reference SteinerSteiner, 2014). Some academics claimed that the absence of organized currency cooperation was the primary cause of the world's economic imbalance and the global financial crisis of 2007–2008. (Reference LiuLiu, 2014; Reference Que and LiQue and Li, 2014). As a result, a multicurrency global reserves system was suggested as a post-crisis solution for liquidity surpluses brought on by extremely low interest rates. This would also lessen reliance on the US dollar (Reference XiangXiang, 2014).

The creation of a dominant currency and the change from one dominant currency to another historically have not been the product of either unilateral or cooperative efforts by states. For instance, the Bank of England's advocacy did not result in the Dutch guilder's demise as the predominant currency in Europe. Instead, the Bank of Amsterdam suffered from policy insolvency, which meant that the net worth was negative under its policy objectives, and as a result, the guilder lost its position as a reserve currency. (Refer to Stella and Lönnberg.) Quinna and Roberds, Reference Stella and Lönnberg, 2008 (2016) Quinna and Roberds. In a similar vein, the Bretton Woods Conference recognized the US dollar's position as the world's reserve currency without the US government forcing it upon other nations (see Eichengreen and Flandreau). (2008) Eichengreen and Flandreau. Due to Japan's economic stagnation since the 1990s, the Japanese government's attempts to internationalize the yen through a variety of mechanisms, such as creating an offshore market and increasing Japan's foreign assistance using the yen, failed (Reference Wu and WuWu and Wu, 2014). It has also been debated how dominant the US dollar is compared to other emerging foreign currencies. There are currencies that are becoming more influential in global monetary matters and could pose a threat to the dollar's hegemony. The euro is one of them, and the yuan is the second. Footnote3 The ability of the euro and renminbi to overtake the dollar as the next dominant world currency is, however, limited by their inherent flaws. Despite being the second-most significant global currency after the US dollar, the euro's international position has largely remained unchanged over the past 20 years. The euro is unable to question the dollar's hegemony in the international financial markets because the euro financial market is smaller and less developed than the market for assets denominated in dollars. The scale and sophistication of the renminbi's financial market are inferior to those of the dollar. The absence of unrestricted foreign capital flows is an additional issue. As a result, academics have generally concurred that the US dollar continues to be the dominant currency in the world and that no other currencies have yet effectively challenged it (Reference Helleiner and Kirshner). Helleiner and Kirshner (2009); Eichengreen (2012) (Reference). The mechanisms and potential outcomes of the BRICS countries' joint de-dollarization efforts have not yet been adequately explained by existing research due to the lack of a historical model for a rising power alliance.

Prior studies have revealed a wide global trend toward the dedollarization of the financial sector, which began in the early 2000s and persisted through the global financial crisis. With only a few exceptions, including Peru, this trend has usually stopped or even turned around in many nations (Reference Cato and TerronesCato et al., 2016). The dedollarization efforts of nations that are subject to US sanctions, as well as the effects of these efforts on US foreign policy and the international monetary system, have been the focus of recent research on economic statecraft. Scholars disagree regarding the long-term effects of these individual de-dollarization initiatives on the US dollar's dominance and on the global currency system, despite the fact that they agree that countries subject to US sanctions have a common incentive to de-dollarize their cross-border settlements (Reference Mathews and Selden). Mathew and Selden, 2018; McDowell, 2020; Andermo and Kragh; Reference Kragh and Andermo, 2021). Despite the expanding theoretical and policy discussions on de-dollarization, coalitional de-dollarization efforts carried out by a driven group like BRICS have not been thoroughly examined in the literature. It has consequences for policy as well as theory to fill this gap in the existing literature. US policymakers risk ignoring and underestimating coalitional threats to the US's position as the world's financial leader if they are unable to fully comprehend the developing de-dollarization coalitions.

The rising power coalitions and incumbent power dichotomy has been the main focus of recent international relations writing on rising power coalitions. Rising powers aim to elevate their position and power as global governance agenda- and norm-setters in this context. Footnote4 From the standpoint of hard security, an alliance is usually defined as a "formal association of states for the use (or non-use) of military force, under certain conditions, against states outside their own membership" (Reference SnyderSnyder, 1997, p. 4). According to recent research, emerging powers create flexible alignments rather than security-focused alliances and are unlikely to pursue military alliances to challenge US leadership because they are economically and financially ingrained in the current system (Reference ChidleyChidley, 2014; Reference Han and PaulHan and Paul, 2020). Some academics contend that rising powers used soft balancing or "nonmilitary instruments to delay, frustrate, and undermine" US global leadership in the absence of hard balancing and military threats from emerging powers (Reference PapePape, 2005). These issues eventually depend on the goals of emerging powers and whether they are reformers, status quo powers that prioritize reform, revolutionaries, counterrevolutionaries, or logical revisionists (Reference LiptonLipton, 2017; Reference DreznerDrezner, 2019).

The circumstances under which a coalition of rising powers would seek different counter-hegemonic strategies have been theorized in existing scholarship. The coalition can oppose the current administration by adopting a "go-it-alone" (Reference GruberGruber, 2000) strategy: its members could exclude the US and work outside of the current framework, thereby restricting US policy options rather than pressuring or persuading the US to alter its behavior. States will be motivated to establish new institutions in areas where the preferences of the incumbent and the rising powers diverge because these are the areas where existing international institutions are likely to face challenges (Reference HenningHenning, 2017; Reference Stephen and Parzek 2019 (Stephen and Parzek). A growing power coalition can use institutions and markets as the two arenas for action when exercising collective financial statecraft, and it can make changes to the current system or create brand-new, rival structures (Reference)

Roberts, Armijo, and Katada References: Katada, Roberts, and Armijo (2017); Kruck and Zangl 2020 (Kruck and Zangl). Scholars discussed the fundamental choice of operating inside versus outside the system, even though they did not define how a rising power coalition can challenge the dollar hegemony.

Prior research has examined rising powers' institutional choices, such as creating new institutions and trying to reform important existing institutions, in the context of their coalitional counter-hegemonic challenges.

Footnote5 For instance, the China-led Asian Infrastructure Investment Bank (AIIB) is a prime example of counter-hegemonic institutionalism because it exemplifies rising powers' resentment of US-led multilateral institutions and their disagreements with the United States regarding international economic governance (Reference Ikenberry and Nexon). 2019 (Ikenberry and Nexon). Less has been said about the "market choices" of rising powers and the applicability of the status quo of market tools for coalitional mobilization. Existing literature has shed light on how self-executing contracts built on blockchain could be used to accomplish trade dedollarization among small groups of nations, like the BRICS (Reference AggarwalAggarwal, 2020). Cryptocurrencies and currency swaps may also be used to dedollarize the world's oil commerce (Reference LadasicLadasic, 2017). However, the methods by which a broad coalition for de-dollarization could be organized and how such a coalition could achieve economies of scale have not been methodically assessed in these proposals. As a consequence, the issue of monetary alliances between emerging powers has not been addressed in existing literature. Therefore, it runs the risk of underestimating the coalitional breadth and credibility of an alliance of rising powers, particularly if its members have similar grievances with the dollar and possess the financial means to establish their own markets and institutions.

In the early literature on BRICS' collective financial statecraft, the issue of whether BRICS can limit the dollar's "exorbitant privilege" has garnered attention. Reference Papa and Bruetsch In their 2013 study of BRICS associational dynamics in the currency space, Bruetsch and Papa discovered that while BRICS produced shared narratives to lessen the privilege of the dollar, its members' conflicting interests and disagreements over potential remedies undermined coalitional efforts. After that, academics assessed BRICS' effectiveness as a financial alliance and as a force for mass action. Most significantly, BRICS has taken the lead among emerging markets in altering the global financial system by creating substitute sources of emergency aid and development funding in order to establish a framework that better serves its objectives and ideologies (Reference). Hanemann and Huotari References Huotari and Hanemann (2014), Drezner and Drezner (2019), Kring and Gallagher, and 2019 (Kring and Gallagher). Although scholars concur that BRICS financial cooperation is growing, they disagree about the likelihood and legitimacy of BRICS initiatives to change the current global system. While some question BRICS' ability to change the global economic system, others believe that BRICS' format as an informal organization may enable it to amass significant power (Reference Cooper and Farooq). (2013) Cooper and Farooq. Reference By presenting evidence to show that it is possible for the BRICS to "take advantage of a fragmented and disparate global economic governance environment to leverage benefits" under particular circumstances, GallagherGallagher (2015) reconciled these scholarly differences.

The capacity of BRICS to build a strong coalition is a requirement for presenting itself as a credible de-dollarization coalition. Although the strength of BRICS' collective de-dollarization initiatives has not been openly discussed in the literature, it has been demonstrated that BRICS has engaged in "collective financial statecraft" to undermine the current liberal international order (Reference Roberts, Armijo and KatadaRoberts et al., 2017). The joint mobilization of the BRICS to change global financial governance is best seen in organizations like the NDB and the CRA (Reference ChinChin, 2014; Reference Biziwick, Cattaneo, and Fryer). References: Biziwick, Cattaneo, and Fryer (2015); Qobo and Soko References include Qobo and Soko from 2015, CooperCooper from 2017, and Suchodolski and Demeulemeester. Demeulemeester and Suchodolski, 2018). As the foundation for larger developing-country coalitions to challenge US hegemony, BRICS has not only changed conventional power structures within the current system, such as the World Trade Organization (Reference HopewellHopewell, 2017).

Other academics have a more negative view of the gathering of the BRICS. According to some, BRICS is unlikely to develop into a credible anti-Western coalition that can seriously challenge US leadership and alter the current international order (e.g., Reference LuckhurstLuckhurst, 2013). The political, economic, and ideological diversity of BRICS may limit the group's ability to alter the current system (Reference Radulescu, Panait, and Voica). Reference TierneyTierney, 2014; Reference LiLi, 2019); the power imbalance within BRICS

(Reference PanditPandit, 2019); and its lack of a collective world order perspective marketable to the larger international community are some of the issues that need to be addressed (Reference NuruzzamanNuruzzaman, 2020). Scholars argue that the disparate development assistance models among individual members could undermine a cohesive BRICS model, even in the area of development finance, which is frequently used as proof that BRICS is a counter-hegemonic group (Reference LiLauria and Fumagalli, 2019). The inability of BRICS to change the global financial order through collective institutional innovation is demonstrated by the group's failed effort to establish its own credit rating agency (Reference Helleiner and WangHelleiner and Wang, 2018).

Last but not least, some studies from the past that looked at BRICS financial cooperation through the NDB and CRA cases assessed the prospects for de-dollarization through these BRICS-governed multilateral financial organizations (Reference ChossudovskyChossudovsky, 2018; Reference KievichKievich, 2018). However, the broad range of de-dollarization initiatives that the BRICS members have tried out have not been fully analyzed by existing study. Furthermore, the "coalitional de-dollarization" of the BRICS has not been thoroughly investigated. A thorough examination of how the BRICS have collaborated with other non-BRICS players to achieve economies of scale for their de-dollarization efforts is also lacking in the existing research.

Despite the fact that BRICS (Brazil, Russia, India, China, and South Africa) developed numerous de-dollarization initiatives to lower currency risk and evade US sanctions, existing research has not methodically examined BRICS as a rising power de-dollarization alliance. This study creates a framework called "Pathways to De-dollarization" to address this gap and uses it to examine the institutional and market mechanisms developed by BRICS countries at the BRICS, sub-BRICS, and BRICS Plus levels. The BRICS de-dollarization coalition's leaders and adherents are identified, the coalition's strength is evaluated, and it is determined how BRICS mobilizes other stakeholders. To evaluate BRICS activities from 2009 to 2021, the authors use process tracing, content analysis, semi-structured interviews, archival research, and statistical analysis of quantitative market data. They discover that the coalitional de-dollarization efforts of the BRICS have created vital foundations for a potential alternative non-dollar global financial system.

Will the USD increase once more?

The US currency has had a very stressful year. In fact, the U.S. dollar indicator (USDX), which gauges how the dollar performs against a weighted basket of rival currencies like the euro, yen, pound sterling, Canadian dollar, Swiss franc, and Swedish krona, has surged to levels last seen in May 2002. Additionally, the yield advantage that the United States holds over other major economies in the face of a deteriorating global economic environment may well support the dollar for a number of months to come. This is because the outlook for global growth has recently become highly unstable. However, the aggressive cycle of monetary tightening that the Federal Reserve System (the Fed) is still enacting to rein in runaway inflation is raising important concerns about when the greenback's rally will eventually lose steam.

Early in November, the Fed authorized raising its federal funds rate benchmark for a fourth time in a row by 75 basis points. It is anticipated that the Fed will maintain this rapid upward trend during its upcoming rate-setting meetings. The Fed's recent steadfast commitment to fulfilling its primary mandate of bringing inflation down to its goal level of 2 percent is highlighted by the strong tightening. To accomplish its inflation goals, the central bank must be willing to sacrifice growth and perhaps a sizable number of American jobs. In fact, even if a recession occurs, the Fed will reportedly continue raising rates if doing so will eventually result in sufficiently bringing inflation under control.

Jerome Powell, the chair of the Fed, has openly acknowledged this unfavorable fact. As the Fed continues its monetary tightening, "the odds of a soft landing are likely to diminish," Powell said following September's third 75-basis-point rate increase. Nobody can predict whether this process will cause a recession or, if it does, how important it will be. He continued, however, that the Fed's decision-makers would only think about stopping rate increases if there was a further slowdown in growth, a "modest" rise in unemployment, and "clear evidence" that inflation is moving in the direction of the 2-percent goal. "We must put inflation in the past. I wish there was an easy method to accomplish that. There is none.

The fact that the conflict in Eastern Europe has not yet come to a clear conclusion may also continue to support the dollar. Given that the US Congress is still largely united in its commitment to continue providing military and humanitarian aid to Ukraine and that Russia has recently increased the number of reservists in its fighting forces by 300,000, the war is certain to continue well into 2023. This unpredictability by itself ought to contribute to the dollar's strength in the upcoming months as the US continues to draw foreign capital seeking protection in the dollar.

However, it also means that the economic sanctions imposed on Russia as a result of the start of the war in late February will continue to be in effect, which could cause energy costs to soar once more. As a result, the risk to the European economies from their inability to meet their energy requirements will continue to be high for the foreseeable future, which will cause the euro to continue to lose value against the dollar and other major world currencies. UBS stated in late September that it was maintaining the euro as the least preferred currency and extending its 0.96 forecast for the euro's value to March 2023.

In spite of several weeks of political turmoil, the situation in the United Kingdom is still perilous. Late in September, investors dumped the British pound sterling (GBP) in reaction to the puzzling tax cuts that the government, led by now-former Prime Minister Liz Truss, forced through at a time of significant hardship across the nation. In fact, the pound's value against the dollar fell to an all-time low of just 1.035. Even though the chaotic Truss regime was overthrown in just 45 days, there are significant doubts about whether the new administration, headed by the former chancellor Rishi Sunak, will help the UK achieve the required recovery. In terms of the GBP/USD exchange rate, one might be inclined to support continued dollar strength, though it must be noted that the pound has made up a significant amount of lost ground recently. Meanwhile, the UK's 10-year gilt yield has trended lower recently as renewed optimism about Sunak's ability to stabilize the markets has increased.

Indeed, as their value against the dollar continues to decline and the probability of a global recession increases, economies around the world may very well experience continued pressure on their currencies. However, the US is anticipated to perform better than many of its advanced economic rivals next year, and the Fed's continued maintenance of high interest rates should encourage more investment into the US and support the dollar's strength. "The Fed hike plus the dollar strength have priced a set of emerging and frontier markets out of the dollar bond market, and they are facing a steady...build-up of pressure," according to Brad Setser, a senior fellow at the Council on Foreign Relations (CFR), who spoke with political news site Grid in late September. "That has been causing a lot of worry."

The US dollar would top at the end of the first quarter of 2023, according to a UBS forecast from late September. And ANZ Bank (Australia and New Zealand Banking Group) believes that the Fed's strong monetary tightening will cause the value of the dollar to peak in the first half of 2019. "In the short term, we see little chance for any immediate relief from USD strength because real yields are so negatively skewed. Accordingly, we anticipate that the USD will deviate from [its] reasonable value as a result of the bank's tightening monetary policy, the economists of the institution wrote on September 27. "As we anticipate that global recessionary worries will worsen in the upcoming months, the US dollar will continue to draw bids from investors seeking safe haven assets. The US Dollar Index (DXY), in accordance with our stronger outlook for the US dollar, is likely to reach its peak at 115 in the first half of 2023.

But not everyone is persuaded that the dollar will continue to appreciate considerably above its current levels, or even that the Fed will keep raising interest rates at its current rate. According to Wells Fargo, the US will experience a slump the following year. The bank predicted in late August that the Fed would reduce interest rates in reaction, which would cause the dollar to retrace its steps and lose ground against other major currencies in 2023. The dollar may therefore reach its peak in the fourth quarter before beginning a "cyclical fall" against other world currencies, according to Wells Fargo's advice to clients. The bank's analysts, under the direction of Nick Bennebroek, predicted that the US dollar would trend lower over the course of 2023 as those rate cuts were signaled, priced, and put into effect. "The greenback should begin a period of cyclical decline against most G10 currencies as well as some emerging currencies next year as interest rate differentials swing back in favor of foreign currencies."

The long-term effects of the de-dollarization process, which several nations have been working on this year, none more so than China, should also not be understated. Late in September, the People's Bank of China requested the largest state-owned banks in the nation to sell dollars in Hong Kong, New York, and London to offset the yuan's 15% decline against the dollar since the year's beginning. Unnamed sources told Reuters that banks were also ordered to review their offshore yuan holdings and make sure their US dollar reserves were prepared for use.

And according to a number of sources, traders saw Chinese banks offloading a lot of dollars on October 26, which caused the offshore yuan to rise by a record 1.8 percent. Bloomberg cites traders who refused to be named as saying the move's strength caught out proprietary desks with stop-loss levels activated. According to Alvin T. Tan, head of Asia strategy at RBC Capital Markets, "there was a major under-performance of the yuan since the congress meeting, and we are seeing a whiplash here as the US dollar tumbles," but he added that further yuan depreciation over the medium term could materialize given China's current growth challenges.

The rapid speed of Federal Reserve interest rate increases is a major factor in the dollar's increase in 2022. The Fed's rate of tightening is likely to slow, giving the dollar room to drop even more in the early 2023 case that central bank policies converge.

By the conclusion of this quarter, analysts and Trading Economics' global macro models predict that the US dollar will be trading at 106.06. Looking ahead, we predict it will sell at 110.80 in a year. In March 2023, Fridays

Although the US dollar has weakened from its apex, due to global macroeconomic uncertainty, exchange rate volatility will still be high in 2023. However, despite the likelihood of further dollar depreciation in 2023, it is anticipated that exchange rate volatility will stay high.